THE KINGDOMS OF KUSH AND AKSUM

Ancient History for Kids
Children's Ancient History

BABY PROFESSOR
EDUCATION KIDS

Speedy Publishing LLC

40 E. Main St. #1156

Newark, DE 19711

www.speedypublishing.com

In this book, we're going to talk about the ancient kingdoms of Kush and Aksum. So, let's get right to it!

WHAT WAS KUSH?

Kush, which had previously been called Nubia, was a kingdom in Africa in ancient times. It was connected to both the history and culture of Ancient Egypt.

Nubia

White Nile

WHERE WAS KUSH LOCATED?

Kush was located in what is now Sudan, a country in the northeastern section of Africa. The major cities of the kingdom were located on the riverbanks of the Nile River and its branches, the White Nile and Blue Nile Rivers.

THE BEGINNINGS OF KUSH

Some of the first people to live in the northern part of Africa were the Nubians. About 3000 BC, they lived in small villages due south of Egypt. It was the perfect location. The soil was fertile and the freshwater from the Nile provided water to drink, fish to eat, and mud to build homes.

Nubians

ancient Nubian tomb

Eventually, the city they built was advanced for its time. The upper class, which consisted of the king and his noblemen, became wealthy through their commerce with Egypt and other surrounding civilizations. The Nubians built ornate tombs for their dead just like the Egyptians.

Over a thousand years of civilization, the Nubians became more powerful. Around 2000 BC, they evolved to become the kingdom of Kush. By trading ivory and other treasures with surrounding civilizations, the citizens of Kush became wealthy.

ancient city of Kush Kingdom

Meroe Pyramids

THE EGYPTIANS CONQUER KUSH

The wealth of the Kushites didn't go unnoticed. The Egyptians saw their growing civilization as a threat so in 1500 BC, they sent their armies to Kush and grabbed control over it. The Egyptian Pharaoh was now their ruler and subsequent pharaohs would rule them for 500 years.

Then, around 1000 BC, the Kushites won their freedom back. In 724 BC, King Piankhi, also called King Piye, trained a large Kushite army and they conquered Egypt and made it their own. The Kushite reign of Egypt wouldn't last for a long time however. Fifty-three years later, a civilization with superior weapons, the Assyrians, would overtake them again.

Assyrian Archer

Assyrian King

THE ASSYRIANS BANISH THE KUSHITES FROM EGYPT

Around 671 BC, the Assyrians raided Egypt. They had weapons made of iron that were stronger than the bronze weapons used by the Kush soldiers. They took over Egypt and sent the Kushites back to the region they had occupied before their civilization had taken over Egypt.

THE GOLDEN AGE OF THE KUSH KINGDOM

The years after they left Egypt were a time of rebuilding for the Kushites. They became prosperous from trade and they built fabulous, ornate homes. Their cities were beautiful and their culture thrived until the Aksums established their kingdom around 400 BC. The Aksums conquered the Kingdom of Kush, 750 years later around 350 AD.

Meroe Pyramids

TWO CAPITAL CITIES

The city of Napata was founded along the Nile in the northern region of the kingdom of Kush. It was the site of the capital during much of the kingdom's golden age. Around 590 BC, the Kushites moved their capital to Meroe, a city that was further south, away from the conflicts with Egypt. The city did a lot of trade in iron and their metalworkers were some of the best in the world at that time.

THE CULTURE OF THE KINGDOM OF KUSH

The Egyptians ruled the Kushites for a long time and their cultures blended in many ways. Their governmental and religious practices were very similar to the Egyptians. They constructed pyramids for tombs as well as worshipped many of the Egyptian gods, although their pyramids were smaller in size.

Statue of the God Anubis

Many of their pyramids were built near Meroe and some still stand today. The Kushites followed the practices of mummification as the Egyptians did, so that bodies would be preserved after death. They had a strong belief in the afterlife. It's possible that the ruling class of Kushites thought of themselves as Egyptians.

There was definitely a social class system in the civilization. The Pharaoh or chief ruler was at the top and was at times considered to be a deity. Many of the Kushite leaders were women, so it was not unusual for the kingdom to have a queen. The priests who conducted temple ceremonies were the next in terms of importance.

Statuettes of Kushite Kings

It was believed that they had a communication system to speak to the gods. Next, were the craftspeople, like the artisans who fashioned gold and iron. This type of metal working talent was prized and rewarded. Scribes were respected as well since they were able to read and write and maintain a history of the kingdom.

Most people in the kingdom were farmers. They grew the grains of barley and wheat. They also grew crops of cotton, which was used to create fabric for clothing. The lowest social classes were the slaves and laborers. The life expectancy for all adults in Kush was about 25 years of age.

BUILT UPON
GOLD AND IRON

The land of the kingdom of Kush was rich in both gold and iron. Gold was prized for jewelry and other decorations and could be traded to the Egyptians and surrounding nations. Iron was another very important asset. It was used to make the sturdiest tools as well as military weapons.

These assets helped the kingdom become very wealthy. Ivory was important as well. Feathers and animal hides were traded and so was incense. Slaves were bought and sold for wealthy households.

Aksum Ruins

WHAT WAS AKSUM?

Like Kush, Aksum was an ancient civilization in the continent of Africa. The kingdom was also called Axum and eventually it was named Ethiopia.

WHERE WAS AKSUM LOCATED?

Most of the kingdom of Aksum was located in the Horn of Africa. The kingdom's lands were located along the western bank of the Red Sea. However, at different times in its history it also ruled over lands that were situated along the eastern bank.

Ruins in Aksum

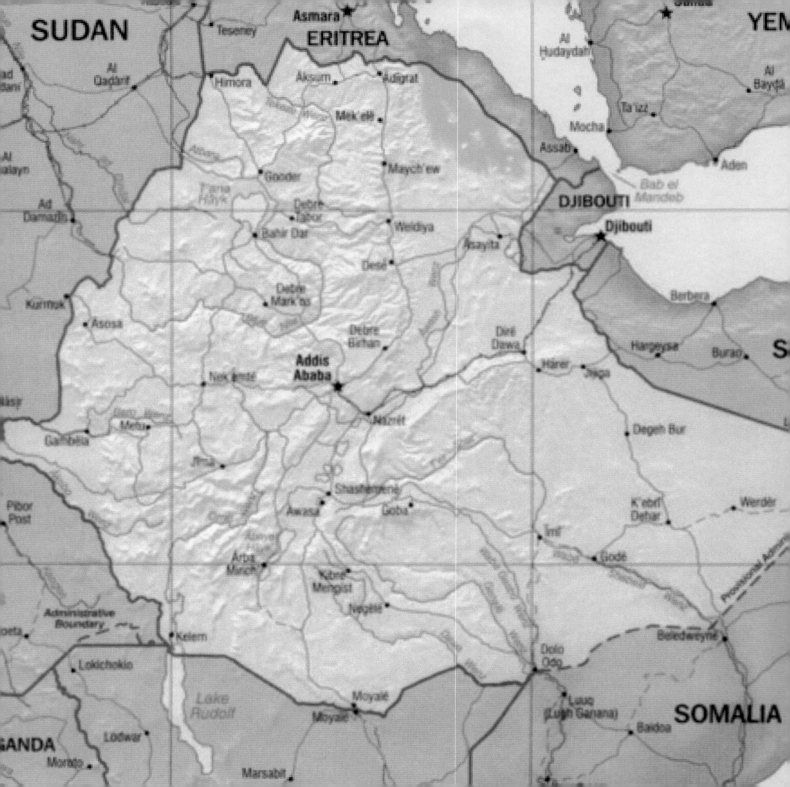

A map of the kingdom of Aksum would overlap the present-day country of Eritrea as well as the northern part of what is now known as Ethiopia. The countries of Sudan, as well as Yemen and the southern portion of Saudi Arabia would be covered by ancient Aksum as well.

THE BEGINNINGS OF AKSUM

The kingdom of Aksum was founded around 500 BC. However, it wasn't until 100 AD when it became a power base. It reached its height between 325 AD to 360 AD under the rule of King Ezana. The kingdom remained in power until 960 AD when it was overthrown by a queen from a foreign land.

Axumite Palace

Nile River

THE KINGDOM OF AKSUM

The people of Aksum held a strip of important territory along the Red Sea. Once they had defeated the Kingdom of Kush in 350 AD and burned the city of Meroe to the ground, they had the iron and gold of the Kushites and the transportation along the Nile River.

They now controlled the ports into and out of Africa. Ships from the countries of Italy as well as India and Persia delivered goods to the region and then took ivory, gold, and iron back in trade. The major port was the city of Adulis located right on the coastline of the Red Sea.

Church of St. Mary of Zion

Around 330 AD a pair of missionaries who were shipwrecked preached their message of Christianity to Aksum's King Ezana. He decided to convert to Christianity and he declared it to be the official religion of the Aksum kingdom. For almost three centuries, the kingdom thrived, but then around 600 AD the Muslims started to steal the kingdom's goods as well as their territories.

The Muslims were a force to be reckoned with, and the kingdom became smaller as their resources were depleted. The attack continued when the port city of Adulis was destroyed by Muslim invaders in 710 AD. Eventually, the people began to call their kingdom Ethiopia, a name still in use today.

Ruins at Gondar, Ethiopia

The Great Obelisk, Aksum

THE CULTURE OF THE KINGDOM OF AKSUM

Because Aksum was an important center of trade in the region, it became a "melting pot" of cultures. Greek became the language of trade. The kingdom of Aksum became one of the most powerful and advanced civilizations of that time period.

They had their own written language and were able to mint coins from gold and other metals. Because much of their land was mountainous slopes, they developed ways to farm it with terraces and advanced irrigation methods.

Bath of the Queen of Sheba

Their style of architecture didn't include pyramids, but they did have stelae like the Egyptians. These are upright stone slabs that have incriptions as well as decorative doors and windows on them. The tallest of these stelae were about 100 feet in height. The most famous of these structures is called the Obelisk of Aksum. When Italian soldiers marched into Ethiopia in 1935, they took the pieces, but it was reconstructed in 2008 and returned to its rightful place.

Awesome! Now you know more about the ancient kingdoms of Kush and Aksum. You can find more Ancient History books from Baby Professor by searching the website of your favorite book retailer.

Visit

BABY PROFESSOR
EDUCATION KIDS

www.BabyProfessorBooks.com

to download Free Baby Professor eBooks
and view our catalog of new and exciting
Children's Books

Made in the USA
Monee, IL
02 December 2020

50635372R00040